TO WHOM IT MAY CONCERN...

ESSAYS FOR EDUCATORS BY EDUCATORS

EDITED BY

SARAH-JANE THOMAS, PHD

EDITED BY

NICOL R. HOWARD, PHD

CONTENTS

FOREWORD

To Whom it May Concern...

...the purpose of this project was to connect *two* Master's level classes from *two* education programs, in *two* universities, on *two* opposite sides of the country. The two professors connected in 2014 through social media, and became fast friends and frequent collaborators. Over five years, they worked on numerous projects together including edcamps, blog posts, and even a book series, although they did not meet in person until two years into their work.

This is the power of social media. **This** is the power of connection. **This** is the privilege of teaching in 2019, when we have the power to connect our learners, despite the borders of time and space.

In this book, you will read the words of <u>our</u> learners, most working as in-service teachers themselves. The value of peer-to-peer learning cannot be understated. We hope that through these chapters, you will find helpful information to will enhance your teaching and learning.

We have organized this anthology into three parts:

1. **Letters to the Field:** Lessons learned and advice to other educators and/or Master's students in the field;
2. **Critical Information Literacy:** Ways to help students process information with a critical lens; and
3. **Connection:** Tips to build your PLN (Personal/Professional Learning Network).

At this time, we would like to thank our students who contributed to this anthology, as well as Dr. Kelly Keane and Irene Bal from Loyola University. We would also like to thank you, the reader, and invite you to share out your tips to #TWIMCEDU.

All our best,

Sarah Thomas, PhD and Nicol Howard, PhD

Editors

PART I: LETTERS TO THE FIELD

[1]

BATTLE FOR THE FUTURE

KAT BEATTY

When I first decided to become an elementary school teacher, my only frame of reference for the profession was what I had experienced as a young student living in Texas in the '80s and '90s. From what I remembered, it was a lot of reading from books and trying to listen while being lectured at. All that other stuff—the philosophies, dealing with racial inequities, income disparity, confronting "isms"—was a job for administration to worry about because I don't remember teachers dealing with any of that. I thought I'd just be the underpaid troop in the trench, dodging bullets and grenades, complaining about the generals in their cushy offices getting paid more for doing less. After all, I've worked jobs before, and this was how they pretty much all went.

Flash forward to today, after several classes, many hours of classroom observation and fieldwork experience, and some teaching under my belt, and I realize how naive I was, how little I understood about the noble profession of teaching. "All that other stuff" will be my job, and the most important part of it. The "how" of teaching is just as necessary as the "what." I've come to realize a few things while on my journey to become an educator. Not only do I need to better understand teaching philosophies and examine how I view students through the lens of my biases, but certain traits are important for teachers to have.

Teaching philosophies are an essential part of education. I've learned a lot about Essentialism (teaching to the test) and Progressivism (teaching to think critically), and I've concluded that Essentialism just doesn't work. I'm an older student, thus a product of Essentialism and "boot-strapping" and I look around at my fellow students, adults much younger than myself, and realize there is a vast difference between how we were raised and educated. Yeah, I pulled myself out of poverty (or I will after I start working). I survived school at a time when Texas was perfecting "teaching to the test" before introducing it to the rest of the US, but I'm at a nice private college working on yet another Master's degree. However, I am fully aware that I am the exception, that my "pulling myself up by my bootstraps" has been nothing more than luck and happenstance – and lots of loans.

As for the "isms," those will also be my responsibility. Those students will be in my care, and I need to advocate for them. Now I know how much racial disparity and income inequality impact students and their learning. Not only do they need a safe environment, but I also need to make sure to check myself and my interactions with them to make sure I am not giving in to my personal biases. In fact, I need to work on digging up those biases, evaluating them, and looking for solutions. All students deserve to have a teacher who cares for them, no matter who they are, where they come from, or any of the other millions of factors that make us all different.

I now firmly believe that teachers need passion for their careers and students. I am a long-time student with multiple degrees pursuing yet another degree, so I have experienced a wide range of teachers, both as a student and as a teacher candidate. The teachers who have made an impact on my life have come from both spectrums of passion: Those who love what they do and those who don't. The educators who are in love with teaching are like bees buzzing around flowering bushes in that they spread that love and passion to their students. I am an avid reader because I had teachers who loved to read. I enjoyed classes about subjects that I was indifferent to because the teachers brought them to life (I'm talking about you, Coach Harding, and your fun Civil Law class). But there is a dark side to education: Teachers who clearly no longer have that passion and love for their careers or students. They are more like vines, spreading their tendrils of bitterness and indifference, choking the passion and exuberance of their students until all that is left are empty husks sitting bored in chairs, watching the clock.

But one cannot teach with passion alone. Teachers who love their jobs are great, but we need knowledge in order to impart knowledge. An educator needs intelligence. We don't need to know everything about everything; in fact, we should be aware of our limitations and find ways to overcome them. I've observed in classrooms where one teacher was solid in language arts, another in math, and the two teachers would move the students from one class to another so each student would get the benefit of both teachers and their masteries. Intelligence is more than book smarts, it's also street smarts, knowledge of self, and the willingness to change when what we are doing isn't working.

Finally, I've come to realize is that there should be a sense of community in education. Community among the teachers, among the students, among the faculty and staff, and among the actual community surrounding the school. I've learned that our goal of educating students isn't just about teaching the curriculum, but about teaching them how to be good citizens in this nation. These kids are going to grow up to be the doctors, lawyers, mechanics, managers, and parents of tomorrow. They need to understand their place in society, all of society, not just the social hierarchy of a contained classroom. As teachers, we need to help students connect what they are learning to their lives and futures so they can become informed citizens, not people who are disconnected from what is happening around them. To do this, teachers need to understand their own place, how their school functions within the neighborhood, and where their support structures are. Teachers must understand the community they are sending their students into in order to better understand their students. After all, the students will reflect that community.

I now understand that I had no clue what I was getting

myself into when I decided to go back to school to become an elementary school teacher, but I'm slowly beginning to get it. As a future advocate and educator of tomorrow's adults, I look forward to learning about them and education just as much as I look forward to teaching those kids.

[2]

BUILDING BLOCKS OF A NEW NATION: A FIELDWORK REFLECTION

JENNIFER M. ROWLETT

The walls were bare except for the staple-punctured butcher paper that indicated posters and student work used to line them. Laptops sat in tall stacks, their wires plugged into charging stations, lights blinking furiously. Mrs. Deen's fifth grade class at Alice Birney Elementary School had been state testing all morning and was now relieving their stress at recess. But Mrs. Deen was still hard at work.

She sorted through her simulation materials: state signs, wooden blocks, imitation money, graphic organizers, and scaffolding worksheets. As she set-up state signs on the grouped desks in the classroom, she explained her Articles of Confederation lesson to me.

"I found it on Pinterest about ten years ago and have been using it ever since. The kids love it! You'll see. The chaos will be epic." The words "epic chaos" made me grin; I was excited to observe a classroom lesson that encouraged disorder and raucous behavior after witnessing the complete opposite for a majority of my fieldwork.

After morning testing each day this week, Mrs. Deen's fifth graders had been going over the American Revolution and the Articles of Confederation, ensuring students had enough prior knowledge to build on "to *produce* rather than *reproduce* knowledge" (Levstik & Barton, 2015). This simulation had been scheduled to challenge students to critically think about the weaknesses of the Articles of Confederation and the reasons why the framers decided to write the Constitution.

"I'm going to be the United States and my daughter will be Great Britain," Mrs. Deen explained. "Great Britain's role is to undermine the United States at every turn in the simulation." Mrs. Deen began tossing blocks into a bag.

"I spent the morning grouping the students into five states. I've chosen a responsible student to be Delaware, because she's going to help me get the ball rolling. And then I've split the other students among the other four states. I had to think about which students were leaders and which were followers and divide them evenly."

I looked at the roster she had written out and nodded at the intentionality in her planning. By pre-grouping, Mrs. Deen was not only maintaining the integrity of the simulation she had perfected over the years, but also adapting the simulation to her class's personalities.

Just as Mrs. Deen threw the last block into the bag, the bell rang, signaling the end of recess and the beginning of a lesson I was sure would challenge the ideals of the conventional Essentialist classroom (Mirci, 2016). Mrs. Deen walked outside to greet her students and explain their tasks before they entered. She clarified and repeated instructions when it seemed some students were still confused, and then she read off the roster, and the students took their seats at their state's table.

Each of the five table groups represented a state: Delaware, Connecticut, Pennsylvania, New York, and Virginia. These chosen states represented the thirteen united colonies under the Articles of Confederation. Each state was composed of a different number of students. The number of states and the number of students in those states fluctuate depending on the population of the class. Typically, however, Delaware is represented by one delegate, Virginia represented by eight delegates, and the rest of the states fall somewhere in between those numbers.

Each state was given a bag of blocks: Delaware given the least and Virginia given the most. Each state was also given a stack of imitation dollar bills, this time with Virginia given the least and Delaware given the most. Mrs. Deen gave the groups a few minutes to complete their objective: build the largest and strongest fort. As foreseen, this task was most difficult for Delaware, who only had three blocks to work with. Mrs. Deen used this moment to explain that as states under the Articles of Confederation, they could propose new laws to assist them in their objective. However, the Articles of Confederation did provide some stipulations for this procedure, two of which Mrs. Deen stressed: 1) Each state gets one vote regardless of size, 2) A proposal becomes law only if four out of five states agree.

Mrs. Deen then prompted Delaware to propose the first law that would bring the simulation to a rolling boil. "I propose that states should share blocks!" The larger states reacted immediately to Delaware's proposal, "If we give away our blocks, then we won't win!" Delegates deliberated amongst themselves for a while, thinking of strategies that would increase their block quota and thus produce a larger and sturdier fort. When asked to vote "aye" or "nay," the nays claimed the majority vote, with Delaware the only aye.

It was now time for Great Britain to begin sailing through international waters with her large recycled bag of blocks. She approached Delaware first, preying on the tiny state's recent Congressional loss. "Your vote doesn't matter. You only have three blocks. How are you possibly going to compete with these other larger, more powerful states? But you do have money, so for a fee and the formation of an alliance, I will give you more blocks to work with." The devil on Delaware's shoulder won, and an alliance was formed between Delaware and Great Britain. Not long after, the small state of Connecticut followed suit.

Pennsylvania and New York spotted trouble on the Eastern horizon and formed a military alliance to guard against insurrection. Virginia joined as well. Yet even while these states were trying to maintain their independence from

Great Britain, the temptation of a larger, stronger fort was overwhelming. Great Britain continued to make deals on the side, while the United States blustered about. "You can't do that?! We're an independent nation! Stop cutting deals with my states!"

"Make me," Great Britain egged.

"I will! I have an army!" the United States began passionately, but then trailed off as she remembered a crucial detail, "That I can't pay or clothe or feed, because no one pays me taxes…"

Great Britain smiled smugly and continued to throw her weight around. Each deal she made gave her more power over each state until she controlled the vote in four out of the five states, Pennsylvania the only state continuing to uphold the ideals of the American Revolution. "AMERICA!" they chanted in unison. But their chants were soon stifled by Great Britain's proposal to begin another war. Because Great Britain controlled the majority vote, the only nay was from Pennsylvania. The war was waged between Great Britain and Pennsylvania, and Great Britain won because the United States could not raise a substantial army. The simulation ended with the devolution of the states back into colonies controlled by Great Britain, as if the American Revolution had never been fought.

The United States became Mrs. Deen again, and she instructed her students to write a reflection on the simulation. "Summarize what happened and then analyze what your state could have done differently to produce your desired outcome." Students discussed the simulation in their state groups and then began writing.

"What if the states had accepted Delaware's proposal and voted to share blocks? How would that have changed things?" Delaware wrote that she should have "been eloquent with the states to persuade them all to unite as one to fight off Great Britain." Other students were able to recognize that their "vote was not enough." By engaging in "imaginative entry," Mrs. Deen's students were able to "imagine the perspective of participants from another time and place without imagining beyond their data" (Levstik & Barton, 2015). This empathy allowed the students to understand the framers' dilemmas in context and critical think accordingly. It also enabled students to make the connection between historical agency and their own civic engagement.

Mrs. Deen's simulation was an effective way to embed thinking skills into the social studies unit, as well as engage students in collaborative, disciplined inquiry. Students gained a more in-depth understanding of the weaknesses of the Articles of Confederation because they were "doing history" by developing their own ideas, rather than merely recounting history by memorizing the teacher's ideas (Levstik & Barton, 2015). It is only through this authentic, interactive engagement with social studies can we as educators teach the subject effectively.

References

Levstik, L. & Barton, K. (2015). *Doing history: Investigating with children in elementary and middle schools.* New York: Routledge.

Mirci, P. (2016, February). *Identifying the core philosophies of education.* Unpublished manuscript, University of Redlands.

PART II: CRITICAL INFORMATION LITERACY

[3]

DIGITAL LITERACY: NOT JUST FOR CHILDREN

SAMANTHA BAKER & KATIE BOLGER

Digital literacy is a relatively new term in today's world. "Literacy" itself can be "generally referred to as reading and writing skills. Digital literacy is the ability to use information and communication technologies to find, evaluate, create, and communicate information, requiring both cognitive and technical skills," according to the article "What is Digital Literacy" from edweek.org (Heitin, 2018). As children, we grow up learning how to read and write, as well as do other daily living skills. Now, we live in a society where technology is more prevalent and the expectations of what we are learning, specifically related to technology, are increased. We also find ourselves having to continually be up-to-date with the most recent technologies to navigate our changing world.

NETIQUETTE

Digital literacy can come in many forms and across a variety of platforms. In today's society, we need to transcribe our reading and writing skills to online text and apply our background knowledge to many media topics and opinions. We need to "decode" text that has abbreviations or other meanings. We see new forms of communication and connections through memes, hashtags, and other new "slang."

A new term has been developed: "netiquette," as described by Google's (2018) online dictionary is "the correct or acceptable way of connecting on the internet." As the need for digital literacy increases, there is also an increasing need to teach students how to differentiate reliable online sources from unreliable sources and which sources are the most relevant for projects or assignments they may be working on. Due to the need for all of these areas of digital literacy to be addressed in the classroom, teachers are being expected more and more to incorporate digital literacy and digital citizenship into students' daily instruction and across all curricular areas.

DIGITAL LITERACY AND EQUITY

One issue we face, especially as educators, is the need to teach our students digital literacy. In schools, we do not always have the resources we need, such as computers for each student, or even access to a class set of computers every week to consistently teach digital literacy to our students. Some schools even struggle with getting a reliable internet connection, which greatly hinders an educator's ability to teach students digital literacy effectively.

Beyond equity issues that affect our abilities to effectively teach digital literacy to students, district mandates affect our ability to teach digital literacy as well. There are rules or policies that each county has in place for students using devices or bringing their own devices onto school properties. In the article "A New Digital Literacy," Carolyn R. Pool (2017) discusses the importance of a school in Raleigh having a computer for every teacher so that the teachers could become digitally literate, even before having the funding for a computer for each student. The article goes on to further talk about funding technology in other countries in which the distribution of computers is minuscule.

Pool's article concludes by saying that computers combined with experienced teachers can create the possibility of global "internet-based" instruction. In this theory, a school's best teacher can become available to anybody on the net. We can use this technology to communicate with classmates and teachers through emails, chat lines, and other electronic forums. Teachers can use the internet to their advantage and reach others on a global level. This could be incorporated by having classes connect with each other across the world and make learning more engaging for students when they have the change to connect with others and share their ideas beyond their immediate community. We believe that once the connection is made between the online teacher and learner, the possibilities are endless.

IS DIGITAL LITERACY JUST FOR KIDS?

Another issue involving digital literacy was brought up by an Edutopia article titled, "Why media literacy is not just for kids" (Boss, 2011). In this piece, the author explains that students know how to navigate the web and post on social media, but there are some other skills they may be missing. Students may not have the knowledge needed to write a thoughtful letter to an editor, voice their opinion on a call-in radio show or access local media to advocate for community action. These are also important forms of digital literacy. Again, as teachers, we need to take digital literacy to a deeper level. The article discusses getting the communities involved and using many of our resources so people of all ages can benefit from learning more about digital literacy.

THE IMPORTANCE OF DIGITAL LITERACY SKILLS FOR ALL

In schools and districts across the country, there is an emphasis on the need to teach students digital literacy skills. According to Prensky (2001), children in today's society have grown up in the digital age and have been exposed to technology, including tablets, computers, TV's, smartphones, and many other devices, for the majority of their lives. Due to this exposure, our students are apt in operating these devices, searching the internet, chatting through instant messaging platforms, amongst many other skills that are utilized in the business world, (Prensky, 2001). These skills will follow them throughout their educational careers and are becoming increasingly necessary for many of today's careers.

For example, we see children as young as 10 months old, not yet speaking clear words, but able to navigate a video on an iPad or cell phone app. Children are exposed to technologies at an earlier age than before. The oldest generations currently living may not have interacted with a screen until they were in college. But what about adults who did not grow up with the same technologies? How is their lack of digital literacy affecting their jobs and their performance at work? What tools are in place to help these adults master digital literacy skills, which many of today's youth already have embedded into their school years?

Many adults, especially those in the older generations who are generally referred to as "silver surfers," face many challenges when working with technology. In his TED Talk, Doug Belshaw (2012) discussed how his grandmother had difficulty navigating a television menu to get to the show she wanted to watch. She needed to ask a family member for help and was overwhelmed when all of the options and controls were explained to her. If older adults had the same digital literacy skills and understandings as young adults, the older generation might have more success navigating new technology.

HELPING THE "SILVER SURFERS"

Research is continuously showing the need for adults, particularly those over the age of 65, to have the same access to digital literacy skills as today's students. For example, according to "Digital Literacy Initiatives" (2012), "The U.S. Department of Education, Office of Career, Technical, and Adult Education Division of Adult Education and Literacy (DAEL) funds digital literacy initiatives to enable adult learners to succeed in a range of academic activities, including STEM and college and career readiness." The DAEL provides information for adults on finding local literacy programs for basic education, adult secondary education, computer literacy and English as a second language. They have programs that provide low-cost internet access and hardware for their homes, and there are resources for teachers and professionals who interact with adult learners to help improve their use of technology and communication with others.

Other benefits of these adults being digitally literate could include building a sense of community, entertainment such as using a Kindle or streaming TV shows, practical use such as transportation, and even access to health records and data that these adults may not have had as much access to in the past. In 2009, the Obama administration granted an increase in funding for broadband infrastructure, computer centers, and training programs, which have been put to great use in the San Francisco area. These centers offer technology training across 54 locations in low-income housing and senior centers.

The classes offered through this training include teaching elderly citizens "basic computer skills to internet safety to fancy software, with examples of topics including Google Maps, typing, online coupons, Skype, YouTube, Craigslist, social media, graphic design, video editing, and more,"

(Institute of Aging, 2016). In the article previously cited, San Francisco specifically has seen the need to provide adults with the same technology education and training that our students are receiving in schools. They believe in being "caregivers" to our aging loved ones and has provided their citizens with the tools they need to be successful in a digitally literate society, especially with the examples listed above. By providing these opportunities for exposure to these various platforms for communication, those from the silver surfer generation are less likely to suffer from depression, according to a study completed by Michigan State University, the University of Montevallo, Harvard University, and the Phoenix Centre for Advanced Legal and Economic Public Policy Studies in the US (National Health Service, 2014). Many people fear that online communication may cause individuals to become isolated from the world around them, but we believe that providing these opportunities through technology expands one's network and enhances their sense of belonging.

CONCLUSION

As we have seen, the need for digital literacy in society has dramatically increased as technology continues to change. Students have an advantage and can receive digital literacy education embedded in their school day. Students are also growing up in a technologically advanced world and are extremely familiar with the various technologies available to them. We can conclude that adults who did not have the same advantages growing up are beginning to fall behind colleagues in their careers and aren't necessarily equipped with the same skills to function adequately in society. When adults are provided with the same tools and strategies to enhance their digital literacy skills that today's students receive, the possibilities of how our world can advance are endless.

References

Boss, S. (2011, January 19). Why media literacy is not just for kids. Retrieved from https://www.edutopia.org/blog/media-digital-literacy-essential-all-citizens-suzie-boss

Digital Literacy Initiatives. (2017, October 12). Retrieved from https://lincs.ed.gov/state-resources/federal-initiatives/digital-literacy

Heitin, L. (2018, March 01). What is digital literacy? Retrieved from https://www.edweek.org/ew/articles/2016/11/09/what-is-digital-literacy.html

Institute of Aging. (2016, August 03). Empowering a modern life: Improving senior digital literacy in San Francisco. Retrieved from https://blog.ioaging.org/technology/improving-senior-digital-literacy-san-francisco/

National Health Service. "Silver surfers" may have lower depression risk. (2014, April 22). Retrieved from https://www.nhs.uk/news/cancer/silver-surfers-may-have-lower-depression-risk/

Pool, C. R. (November 1997). A new digital literacy: A conversation with Paul Gilster. *Integrating Technology into Teaching, 55*(3). Retrieved from http://namodemello.com.br/pdf/tendencias/tecnolnocurric.pdf

Prensky, M. (October 2001). Digital natives, digital immigrants. *On the Horizon, 9*(5). Retrieved from https://www.marcprensky.com/writing/Prensky%20-%20Digital%20Natives,%20Digital%20%20Immigrants%20-%20Part1.pdf

TED. (2012, March 22). Doug Belshaw: The essential elements of digital literacies [Video file]. Retrieved from https://www.youtube.com/watch?v=A8yQPoTcZ78

[4]

STUDENT-CREATED WEBSITES: WHAT ARE YOU WAITING FOR?

DAVID FITZSIMONS

WHY WEBSITES?

One of the most critical skills that students learn and hone throughout their lives is how to write. This begins in kindergarten with invented spellings and heavy use of illustrations to help tell the story and ideally continues through high school, college and beyond. This regular practice with writing dovetails beautifully with students' growing reading capabilities and the two feed into each other. Reading helps students build their vocabularies and see examples of quality writing from established authors, giving them ideas for use in their own writing. Through writing, students develop their own voice and gain a deeper understanding of the structure inherent in a written document, which increases their ability to understand and navigate complex texts.

As we as educators begin to confront the issue of digital literacy and how to help our students grow as savvy digital consumers, I believe students should also be given ample opportunities to create online content. There are numerous avenues a student can take to work toward this goal, but I'll focus on a particular one in this chapter - creating websites. I love teaching students to create websites, and I'll share some specific experiences below. The names have been changed to protect student privacy, but the stories are real. There is any number of excuses one can make for shying away from a project like this, but I hope to convince you that the impact on students is real, and it's actually not at all difficult to do.

I have helped students create websites for a few different reasons. Officially I am our school's Middle School Math Teacher, but every teacher at our school wears multiple hats. I have taught eighth-grade science as well as electives that run the gamut from flag football to the Age of Exploration to Dungeons and Dragons. In addition, one of my school's key ongoing structures is the requirement that every student complete a self-directed long-term project during each year of middle school. The student chooses the topic of the project and the general goals and works with an advisor to flesh out the specifics.

CREATING A WEBSITE AS A LONG-TERM PROJECT

Recently I had a student who was very interested in video games and computers. We were having trouble settling on a project that would interest him enough for long-term study, but that contained enough real meat that it would be a challenging middle school project. He and I eventually settled on the idea of building a game review website from scratch. It was a formidable project for a middle schooler to tackle, but he applied himself in a way he rarely did with traditional classroom work. He was able to proudly display his work at our school's Mind Fair in the Spring.

If you're nervous about the idea of jumping into helping your students code without any experience of your own, there are numerous resources available free on the web. Joe McFerrin's blog post *Web Development in the Classroom: Web Site Building for Kids!* gives an excellent list of resources to work from (McFerrin, 2013). He has put together a catalog of resources that covers web design from its most basic principles to more complicated HTML scripting so that you and your students can find the resources that are most helpful for you. If you are looking for other technology resources to use with kids, he has those as well, including articles about LEGO robotics, coding, and netiquette.

A SPECIAL ENRICHMENT OPPORTUNITY

I also worked with a fourth grader named Kevin who would eventually become one of my middle school math students. At the time that I worked with him, he was getting a special opportunity to do some technology work. Kevin was the type of student who finished his work quickly but had trouble occupying himself constructively once he had done so. During some of my free periods, I helped him learn to create his own sports website where he could write about the basketball teams he was interested in.

If fourth grade sounds young for a project like this, keep in mind that kids always seem to pick up new technologies more quickly than we do as adults. The Goodell Group has a website full of web design tutorials aimed at kids as young as 10 years old (Goodell, 2015). *Lissa Explains it All* is another website specifically designed to teach kids to write HTML from scratch, presented in a very kid-friendly form (Lissa, 2016).

Kevin got to practice writing and engage in an activity that challenged him once his basic work was done, and I got a great chance to build a relationship with a student I would be working with for multiple years. He also developed an understanding of how websites are put together and how to organize his information so that readers could find what they were seeking.

Even with all of the support that's available for learning HTML, some teachers may not feel ready to take on a project of that magnitude. That's fine, as it really isn't necessary to learn any coding skills to put together a website that a student can be proud of. Larry Ferlazzo has written several blog posts that are sure to come in handy. A 2008 piece, for example, offers advice and resources for both students and teachers and links to some helpful free tools (Ferlazzo, 2008). In a similar resource posted on globaldigitalcitizen.org, Lee Watanabe-Crockett offers a more recently updated list of web design tools that are suitable for use in the classroom (Watanabe-Crockett, 2016).

HELPING STUDENTS CURATE A PORTFOLIO OF THEIR WORK

My last story of student web design might be my favorite. Another core aspect of my school's middle school experience is what we call a Presentation of Learning. At the end of each year, each student compiles a portfolio of their work and presents it in front of a panel that includes their advisor, their parent(s) or guardian(s), other community members, and any other guests the student would like to invite. It's an incredible experience the students take very seriously, and they reflect very insightfully about the year that passed and what they are hoping for in the future.

Unfortunately, aspects of the process go beyond challenging to nerve-wracking for some students. Keeping track of papers over the year can be difficult. Even if they are carefully stored, students who struggle with executive functioning or become nervous with public speaking can find it difficult to put their portfolio binder together and then coherently show the contents.

John was just such a student. He struggled through his presentations in his sixth and seventh-grade years. For his eighth-grade year, we tried a new solution — what if John made a portfolio website and presented his work digitally?

In the week leading up to his presentation, I helped John create a simple website with Google Sites. Using a tool like Google Sites made it so that John didn't have to learn any coding — he simply had to create the pages and type what he needed into each one, much as you would with a basic document. We organized it by subject and uploaded scanned PDFs and other artifacts of his work. When the time came to present, John no longer had to flip nervously through a binder to find the right page he was looking for or try to pull work from plastic page protectors with shaky fingers. Being able to click through his website confidently put John at ease. When someone had a question about an assignment, we could all see the work together on the screen and talk about it clearly. It was a brilliant success, and I have taken this approach with other students since.

MOVING FORWARD

If you haven't already, I strongly encourage you to make a website with your own students or challenge a group to take it on as a project. You will be amazed at what they will put together. One simple way to get started as a whole class is to maintain a class website. This works particularly well for younger and middle-grades students. Even in a classroom where most students are not ready to handle creating their own webpages from scratch, kids can get valuable practice and learn 21st-century skills such as uploading media and writing blog posts. They could give updates on the class pet, write a newsletter for parents, or report on a recent field trip or other meaningful activity. What you and your students can do is limited only by your shared imagination.

References

Ferlazzo, L. (2008, December 12). The best ways for students or teachers to create a website. Retrieved from: http://larryferlazzo.edublogs.org/2008/12/12/the-best-ways-for-students-or-teachers-to-create-a-website/

Goodell, J.J. (2015). Welcome to learning HTML for kids. Retrieved from: http://www.goodellgroup.com/tutorial/intro.html

Lissa. (2016). Lissa explains it all: The first and original HTML help just for kids! Retrieved from: http://www.lissaexplains.com/?true=1

McFerrin, J. (2013, August 2). Web development in the classroom: Web site building for kids! Retrieved from: https://www.iwdagency.com/blog/web-development-in-the-classroom-web-site-building-for-kids

Watanabe-Crockett, L. (2016, December 22). 8 Free website creator tools for classroom projects. Retrieved from: https://globaldigitalcitizen.org/8-free-website-creator-tools

[5]

THE RENAISSANCE OF DIGITAL LITERACY

EDWARD SCHULTHEIS

> If you read all the annals of the past, you will find no century like this since the birth of Christ. Such building and planting, such good living and dressing, such enterprise in commerce, such a stir in all the arts, has not been since Christ came into the world. And how numerous are the sharp and intelligent people who leave nothing hidden and unturned: even a boy of twenty years knows more nowadays than was known formerly by twenty doctors of divinity (Schaff, 1916).

As a student of history, it was only natural for me to go back to the 16th century to tackle a 21st-century issue. Of course, also being a theology teacher, I had to bring a theological perspective to the subject. In 1522, Protestant reformer and preacher Martin Luther wrote poetically about the impact that the Renaissance had on the entirety of life for the people living in Europe. He had watched as the Age of Discovery and the Renaissance forever changed the intellectual, religious, scientific, and cultural landscape of Europe in their wakes. And here he was, writing at a time of upheaval throughout Europe as nationalist groups splintered into various Catholic and Protestant factions, each one assured of their divine justification. For Martin Luther though, the Renaissance was a time of hope, where anything was possible for mankind, while a world of knowledge (and salvation) lay at their feet.

As I was putting together a lesson on the Reformation for my students, I was looking through some quotes that I like to include in my teaching. The one that I read, penned by Martin Luther a few years after his writing of the pivotal 95 Theses, struck me in its ability to resonate today. I think of our technological and social renaissance that we are living in today

— where in the span of 60 years, a mere generation, we have come from black-and-white or basic color televisions to curved, razor-thin televisions capable of receiving a seemingly infinite number of channels via satellite, cable, and internet. We have come a long way from Isaac Asimov's (1950) story *I, Robot*, where Asimov provided the quintessential ethics for robots to now where we have artificial intelligence driving our cars, flipping our burgers (Glowatz, 2018) and soon, calling people on the phone (Welch, 2018). Luther's writings seem well suited to the technological renaissance that we are enjoying today. But just like the 16th-century edition, with our renaissance, there is also the danger of upheaval.

TODAY, we take literacy for granted in many ways. The expectation is that students will be able to read and write at specific grade levels throughout their years of schooling. We have books; therefore, students should be able to read them! However, until the advent of the printing press, and specifically the Johannes Gutenberg movable type model, literacy was for the rich and powerful in Europe. The adoption and spread of the printing press in the 15th and 16th centuries directly contributed to the Renaissance and, of course, the message of the Reformation. It is not a stretch to say that without the Gutenberg printing press, the Reformation would not have occurred! Thus, the broad spread of literacy, the lowered costs of books, and ability to reach a wide audience all played into the success of Luther's message — hence the hopes stressed in his writing in 1522.

In very much the same way, I think we take digital literacy for granted too. Nowhere is this on display more than when students are described as digital natives. Whenever a teacher refers to students as digital natives, what they are really conveying is "these kids should get it because they've grown up with it." Unfortunately, this fallacy is dangerous for all involved. Digital literacy is more than just "growing up with it," it is the combination of finding and consuming digital content; creating digital content; and communicating or sharing it (Heitin, 2016).

Every single time we as educators expect our students to do something because they are "digital natives" what we are really doing is highlighting the naivety of our expectations. Just because the printing press was "invented" doesn't mean people were just expected to be able to magically read and write. In much the same way, we should not expect our students to be digitally literate simply because they have grown up with a phone in their pocket.

As people looking back at history, I think most people take a romanticized view of preceding events. We think of the Crusades through the lens of Robin Hood, or movies that dramatize the action. We look at the Renaissance as this beautiful time of exploration, scientific discovery, and humanistic endeavors. We have an American holiday in October devoted to a man who, by many historical accounts, was a genocidal enslaver of humanity. Yet, we continue to romanticize the past. Even here, we talk about the greatness of the printing press and the amazing things it enabled people to do. But, honestly speaking, the printing press begat division and separation. It enabled ideas to be spread, and that can be a dangerous thing.

The same can be said of digital literacy. We romanticize it even today. "Why should a teacher be lecturing when a student can just look up anything they want on Google/Wikipedia?" The ridiculousness of this statement is the naivety, or romanticizing, of the idea that students will automatically look up all the stuff they don't know, that they will know what they are looking for, and that they will use the information correctly. Therefore, I think we as educators need to move beyond the all-encompassing term "digital literacy." It just doesn't say enough of what we need it to say. It is too easy, just like when we call students "digital natives." We need to be deliberate when we are talking about the implications of our words, and what we mean by them. If we learned anything from Martin Luther and the printing press, words matter...immensely.

We need to think about all the things we are asking of our students when we talk about them being digitally literate. Writing emails, recognizing fake news, making videos, digital footprints, digital legalities, and other areas, are all part of what we say when we talk about digital literacy. Technology continues to expand each day, what are students can do expands every year, and what we need them to understand about being digitally literate changes daily. We as educators need to be more deliberate and specific when it comes to what we expect from our students. We can't just expect them to be digitally "literate" because they've grown up with technology. We are being naive, and we are selling their abilities short!

This is indeed a renaissance of digital literacy. Just like Martin Luther wrote before his posting of the 95 Theses, "and how numerous are the sharp and intelligent people who leave nothing hidden and unturned: even a boy of twenty years knows more nowadays than was known formerly by twenty doctors of divinity" (Schaff, 1916). We are truly blessed with students who are sharp, intelligent, and inquisitive. But we can't romanticize the movement, and we can't be naive about their literacies. We as educators must understand the great advantages and pitfalls of the technologies that exist, and help our students leverage them as best as they can. Without the printing press, the Reformation would never have occurred. What will we look back on years from now and wonder, "you know, without those digital tools, that probably would never have happened?" Let's make sure, whatever it is, is for the positive!

References

Assessment & Teaching of 21st Century Skills. (n.d.). Retrieved from http://www.atc21s.org/

Asimov, I. (1950). *I, Robot.* Garden City, NY. Doubleday.

Glowatz, E. (2018, March 5). Robot flips burgers for California restaurant better than a human. Retrieved from http://www.newsweek.com/robot-flips-burgers-california-restaurant-better-humans-830762

Heitin, L. (2016, November 8). What is digital literacy? Retrieved from https://www.edweek.org/ew/articles/2016/11/09/what-is-digital-literacy.html

Schaff, P. (1916). *History of the Christian Church.* Grand Rapids, MI: Scribner.

Welch, C. (2018, May 8). Google just gave a stunning demo of Assistant making an actual phone call. Retrieved from https://www.theverge.com/2018/5/8/17332070/google-assistant-makes-phone-call-demo-duplex-io-2018

PART III: CONNECTION

[6]

THE CHRONICLES OF A FIRST-YEAR TEACHER AND HOW PROFESSIONAL LEARNING NETWORKS HELPED HER SURVIVE

VICTORIA BOROWY

Team Leader: "Are you going to walk out with us?"
Me: "No, go ahead. I'm going to be a minute, I'm just finishing creating resources for the next unit on heroes."
Team Leader: "Please don't stay late, we can look at it during lunch tomorrow."
Me: "I won't, I'll be quick!"
3 hours later.
Janitor: "We are closing the building in an hour."
Me: "Thanks so much."

Does this conversation sound familiar to you? Maybe you were talking as the team leader, or perhaps you were the new teacher. Undergrad may teach you how to plan lessons and reflect on your teaching, but it doesn't prepare you for the obstacles you face during a school day and how most of the planning and grading occurs after school hours. People laugh saying how easy it must be to be a teacher, especially when you have a two-hour break during the school day to prepare for the next day. What they don't realize is the number of meetings teachers attend, the behaviors teachers deal with, and the setup teachers do to ensure a lesson is a success.

From the outside looking in, a teacher's break may seem like the perfect opportunity to grade papers and plan lessons; however, that is far from the truth.

MY SAVING GRACE

My first couple of months as a new teacher I spent hours every single day outside of the workday to ensure I was prepared and organized. Whether I was at school or at home, my job never ended at 4 pm. To this day, my job still doesn't end at 4 pm. However, I have learned how to balance work and manage my time. I owe a lot of the thanks to the professional learning networks (PLN) I belong to. Teachers who join an online community or subscribe to different educational blogs, forums, and podcasts are building professional learning networks (PLN). "PLNs provide instant access to information and connections to thousands of individuals with an array of expertise. A PLN is a system of interpersonal connections and resources that support informal learning" (Trust, 2012).

When I graduated from college in 2013, I wasn't familiar with many social media sites other than YouTube and Facebook. It was my first year of teaching that I learned about Pinterest, Instagram, and Teachers Pay Teachers. A fellow team member was showing me her accounts and how to use them. I was baffled. The amount of resources that each page provided was insane. I felt like Charlie who won the golden ticket to the Chocolate Factory from Roald Dahl's children novel *Charlie and the Chocolate Factory*! All I had to do was type in the unit name or area of focus, and thousands upon thousands of resources came up. Some resources were free of charge, and others cost money to buy. Some met my needs and others I had to tweak. The important piece to the new discovery was that my outside planning went from 4-5 hours down to 1-2 hours. Flanigan (2011) discusses how busy educators, like me, are increasingly turning to PLNs when they want to ask advice, offer opinions, or engage in deep discussions. They are able to share lesson plans, teaching strategies and students' work. It is important because teachers are able to collaborate with other educators across content, grades and departments from other counties, states, and even countries.

There is nothing worse than feeling like you don't fit in during your first year teaching. Your team can be the best team on the planet, but sometimes teammates just don't have the answers that you need to hear. "The most important thing I learned [from my PLN] is that there is a community of enthusiastic amazing educators that are lifelong learners, always evolving their practice and learning from each other" (Trust, 2016). Turning to your PLN gives you the extra support you need to feel confident as a teacher.

DEVELOPING MY PLN

I have always viewed teacher pages on Instagram, YouTube, and Twitter, but never considered creating a page myself. This all changed for me during the year of 2016. Recognizing the importance of technology, I decided to pursue my Master's Degree in Educational Technology at Loyola University. During the first graduate class, my professor asked us to create a Twitter account. I had never used Twitter before, and I was intrigued. I immediately started to follow a variety of educational accounts because I noticed they posted a lot of articles about the latest and greatest in the educational field. I decided to use my account to retweet the different articles that I had read that I found beneficial to the classroom and wanted to share with other colleagues. What I love about belonging to a PLN is the fact that "social networking allows teachers to connect with teachers in other schools. These partnerships are useful as they keep you abreast of changes in curriculum and content in other states and maybe even other countries" (PLB, 2016). Recently I participated in a Twitter Chat with fellow fourth-grade teachers in #4thchat. The topic was about planning and preparing for evaluation. We were reflecting on our past school year and using our reflection to plan for the next school year. There were people from California, Canada, Ohio, and Indiana in the group chat. They were sharing what their county/district implement, and I was very intrigued by how I could incorporate the ideas into my own classroom. They also shared multiple articles through the chat that had questions to help me reflect more on my previous year. I was able to take the questions back to my school and my team and have a discussion with them about the school year.

SHARING IS CARING

I started thinking about how much I have learned from other Professional Learning Networks, and I decided that I had a lot to share and wanted to create my own pages. Pajaron (2013) reports that:

> Harvard scientists are considering that 'sharing discoveries is more efficient and honorable than patenting them.' This idea embodies the true spirit of a successful professional learning network: collaboration for its own sake. As educators, we aim to be connected to advance our craft.

As a new teacher, I strongly believe in sharing resources with other teachers due to the benefits that come with it. I have learned so much from watching other educational videos and love creating videos that show strategies I incorporate into my daily routine.

I began by creating an Educational YouTube Channel (Victoria Chanda) as well as an Instagram page (msbteach3). I use my YouTube page to post videos and screen-casts. The videos I created under my YouTube channel are primarily for professional development purposes. My main professional learning network is my Instagram account. I take pictures of what is happening in the classroom and share them online. This allows colleagues, parents, students, and teachers around the world to view what is happening in the classroom. I also take these pictures and other original pieces of work and upload them to my Pinterest page.

In an article featured on Edutopia, Vega (2013) discusses how PLNs don't just provide teachers with skills and knowledge to improve their teaching practices, but they also provide an ongoing community that values each teacher's experiences and uses those experiences to guide teaching practices and improve student learning. All of the networks I am on have provided me with ideas to try out in my classroom and have helped me grow as an educator. I know I have a lot to offer and hope I can give back to others through my different Professional Learning Networks.

References

Flanigan, R. (2011, Oct). Professional learning networks taking off. *Education Week.* Retrieved from https://www.edweek.org/ew/articles/2011/10/26/09edtech-network.h31.html

Pajaron, T. (2013, Jan). 20 Tips for creating professional learning network. *Classroom Aid: Connect Learning*. Retrieved from http://classroom-aid.com/2013/01/04/20-tips-for-creating-a-professional-learning-network/

Professional Learning Board. (2016). What are the benefits of social networking for teachers? Retrieved from https://k12teacherstaffdevelopment.com/tlb/what-are-the-benefits-of-social-networking-for-teachers/#respond

Trust, T. (2016). Together we are better: Professional learning networks for teachers. *ScienceDirect.* Retrieved from https://www.sciencedirect.com/science/article/pii/S036013151630135X

Trust, T. (2012). Professional learning networks designed for teacher learning. *ISTE*. Retrieved from https://files.eric.ed.gov/fulltext/EJ972454.pdf

Vega, V. (2013, Jan). Teacher development research review: Keys to educator success. *Edutopia*. Retrieved fromhttps://www.edutopia.org/teacher-development-research-keys-success

[7]

PINTEREST: A TOOL OF THE TRADE

MEGHAN PLOFKIN, NINA PAPARAZZO, & BAILEY GREEN

MEGHAN: PINTEREST FOR EDUCATORS

Before I began teaching, I created a Pinterest account and flooded the boards with my topics of interest. Some boards included college dorm ideas, recipes, work-outs, songs, future wedding and baby ideas (because what girl doesn't plan way in advance for these things), and quotes that kept me inspired. Among all of those boards, I had a Teacher board where I compiled all of my great ideas for when I eventually had my own classroom. This board included lesson plans, inexpensive ideas for decorating your classroom, planners, behavior charts, and pretty much anything else a teacher could want all in one place. I knew that one day it would become my toolbox and go-to resource. I knew this before I even walked through the door of my first classroom, before I had even crossed the stage and had my diploma in hand, and before I had even applied for and accepted the job of classroom teacher. Honestly, it was one of the only things about being a teacher that I was spot-on about. Pinterest is my tool-box and go-to resource for so many ideas as a teacher.

Being an educator can be extremely stressful, and there are times when we forget that we are not on an island by ourselves. There is something relaxing and therapeutic about scrolling through Pinterest at the end of a long work day and finding exactly what you need for next week's lesson, or connecting with another teacher who has amazing ideas you can implement into your own classroom right away. I don't see using Pinterest as work and am more likely to commit time to find great pins about education rather than typing out my own lesson plans. Yes, of course, I still make sure to incorporate my own ideas and infuse these lesson seeds with activities that will allow my students to thrive, but I don't have to start from scratch (unless I want to). An infographic by Buck described it best when it showed that Pinterest allows teachers to "curate content, organize ideas, collaborate with others, and use with students" (2012). Pinterest allows educators to collaborate and create new and exciting resources without re-inventing the wheel.

Pinterest also allows educators to organize their ideas into boards. According to an article in BBC Active, "...visual nature of Pinterest makes it easy to rediscover resources we have saved previously and to store them under a relevant topic title" (2010). The boards can be named based on categories so that educators who may follow you can also look at your board based on what they want to find.

As a teacher, I turn to Pinterest countless times during the school year. I know that I can log into my account and find resources for any unit I am teaching, answers to behavioral questions, and guidance from more experienced teachers...and that is sometimes just the reassurance I need.

NINA: PINTEREST FOR STUDENTS

When I first started using Pinterest as a teacher, the first question I asked myself was, "how can this help my students?" With every tech tool teachers decide to pull into our classrooms, we must contemplate this question. As the platform has developed, much more content has flooded into Pinterest, and it is important that teachers educate themselves regarding the possibilities.

Pinterest offers a wide array of opportunities for student use in and out of the classroom. As Eric Sheninger explains in his Edutopia article "Pinterest for Educators," from curating content to teaching digital citizenship, the opportunities within Pinterest are many (Sheninger, 2012). Stephen Abram, a librarian and principal with Lighthouse Consulting Inc., listed over 35 possible uses for Pinterest on his blog, *Stephen's Lighthouse* such as, "have students pin project ideas" or, "have students photojournal on Pinterest" (Abram, 2012). Both are excellent ideas regarding how to engage students on a highly visual platform.

In my classroom, I have students engage on a surface level with Pinterest, and they enjoy it. Our county policies do not allow for seventh-grade students to create an account on Pinterest, so the most our students can do is view boards I create. In my Social Studies classroom, this still provides a wealth of opportunity for students. I can create boards for specific projects with examples, ideas, and possible sites to research. For instance, a major project in the seventh-grade Gifted and Talented curriculum is the National History Day project. I have a board that links to training videos, past project winners, research tips and strategies, and a variety of other tools. Students know they can go to this visual board to explore and find new ideas.

Another amazing tool for students is the content boards for each of our units with interesting, engaging, and fun content for students to explore. My Ancient Greece Board, for instance, provides videos teaching about the Greek Gods, an interactive game teaching about the Olympics, and a variety of other sites students can seek for enrichment.

Students tend to appreciate the visual and interactive layout that Pinterest gives them. While there are varying levels of student engagement (I wouldn't have a third-grade student searching Pinterest because of the occasionally inappropriate content), the tools available to help students learn are many and valuable.

BAILEY: PINTEREST FOR SPECIAL EDUCATORS

So, there I was, a first-year special education teacher, completely lost as to how to handle a student who had completely shut down, refused to go with his class to related arts, and was now perched on top of a sea of desks, mooning me anytime I tried talking to him about what was going on. Yes, I said mooning me. It was an experience, to say the least. However, it was an experience that I remember distinctly, mostly due to the panic that set in when I realized I had no idea how to help this student through the current crisis. After spending four years at a well-known university and earning a degree in teaching, I had no idea how to handle this situation. I realized then that I needed to arm myself with various techniques and ideas on how to handle any situation I may come across as a special educator. With that, came Pinterest.

Up until that point I had only ever used Pinterest to create a secret "Future Wedding" board where I would pin wedding dresses I couldn't afford, and engagement rings fit for a Kardashian. I hadn't thought about using it for work purposes until I realized I needed to see what ideas were out there and what techniques might work for this third grader who was clearly struggling.

Once I started, I couldn't stop. There was so much information and so many places to find it. I couldn't believe it. I began my search to find out more information related to students with Autism and how to best support them when they're experiencing a crisis. However, I soon realized just how much information I could access. Pinterest is an incredible way to access teacher blogs, informational websites, and much more. It's become a portal where I can simply type in a keyword such as "behavior chart" and be flooded with free samples, links to additional websites, and information related to the best ways to implement a behavior chart for various types of students. Madeline Cummings explains in her Slate article, "There's a Big

Hole in How Teachers Build Skills and Pinterest is Helping to Fill It”:

> Pinterest is by no means intensive. It’s not necessarily ongoing. And it’s certainly not a one-stop solution to shortcomings in teacher training nationally. But many teachers like the fact that they can search for exactly what they want to learn- middle school social science lessons, for example—and connect with others who teach the same grades or subjects (Cummings, 2015).

Pinterest has also been a helpful resource when looking into how to set up a classroom for students with various physical and cognitive needs. Teachers are some of the most creative individuals in the world and their ability to create a “new” activity or change their classroom environment to cater to the needs of specific students is incredible. I couldn’t tell you the number of compliments I’ve gotten related to something in my classroom and my response has been, “Pinterest!!! It’s amazing!!”

Pinterest provides special educators and teachers of all content areas the ability to collaborate with their peers in a new and wonderful way. We, as teachers, are no longer limited to what we know, or what we’ve been taught. Pinterest has provided us with access to new and exciting ideas from educators all around the world and, I believe, has played a huge part in creating more engaging and creative teachers as a whole.

References

Abram, S. (2012, February 8). Pinterest and education [Web log post]. Retrieved May 28, 2018, from http://stephenslighthouse.com/2012/02/08/pinterest-and-education/

BBC. (2010). Using Pinterest for education. Retrieved May 18, 2018, from http://www.bbcactive.com/BBCActiveIdeasandResources/UsingPinterestforEducation.aspx

Buck, S. (2012, April 10). 16 ways educators can use Pinterest [INFOGRAPHIC]. Retrieved from https://mashable.com/2012/04/10/pinterest-teachers/#V94XjAFSviqh

Cummings, M. (2015, April 02). There's a big hole in how teachers build skills, and Pinterest is helping fill it. Retrieved from http://www.slate.com/blogs/schooled/2015/04/02/pinterest_and_teachers_how_the_site_is_filling_a_gap_in_teacher_training.html

Sheninger, E. (2012, March 19). Pinterest for educators [Web log post]. Retrieved May 28, 2018, from https://www.edutopia.org/blog/pinterest-for-educators

[8]
TO COLLAB OR NOT TO COLLAB: THAT IS THE QUESTION
ASHLEY CLARK

> "It's not the most important things that we do but it's the people that do it with us." — *Working together to make things happen: JP Cardoso at TEDxBrainport*

HOW IT ALL BEGAN

It was the summer of 2017 when I conducted my very first webinar in my ET662 class, *Technology Leadership and Professional Learning.* The topic was Community Circles (https://tinyurl.com/y8ncvppn). As this was a group project, we all rallied doing research, creating a timeline and basic framework, as well as creating marketing flyers for our webinar time. I thought myself to be social media savvy with interacting on Facebook and Twitter, especially when it came to finding relevant information and people that I could reach out to. This time it was different, though. We were tasked with inviting people to our webinars. I had made (what I thought) was a catchy invitation using the infographic creator Piktochart, and we blasted it all over our social media accounts. The day of, though, only our classmates and two other outside teachers joined.

I know this was our very first webinar and we were technically only doing it for class…but *why couldn't we get anyone else involved?*

After that class concluded in the summer of 2017, I was preparing for my internship for the following spring semester. As part of our internship, we were to build our own personal learning networks, something I hadn't done too much of because I thought I had some decent knowledge for someone who had been on Twitter for a good number of years.

Then it dawned on me. *What have I been using Twitter for?* Social reasons mainly. In college my friends had Twitter, and I engaged with them online but had never really interacted with others that were in the teaching profession. My Twitter use was incredibly superficial. I was only checking breaking news, or someone's thoughts on the latest dance or fashion trends, but I hadn't sought out anything to *feed my teacher soul.*

THE HOOK

As I started moving closer to my internship, I began to get more heavily involved with Twitter, participating in #BMoreEdChats and even participating as a panelist with

EduMatch. What did I learn from the experiences? ***Put yourself out there!*** I learned more about peer coaching and innovation in education by merely being **present** and interacting by answering questions.

Think about that, just *being present.* How many learning opportunities do you think you potentially miss because we are "there" at professional development and not actually listening or engaging? I know what you're thinking but not all virtual (or in person) professional development is boring (no offense to you, mandated PD). The cool thing about virtual or online professional development is that **you** are in control. You are the one that chooses the sessions you want to attend based on **your** interests. I chose the peer coaching Twitter chat and the Innovation in Education EduMatch live episode (https://tinyurl.com/y85k3cjg) because I personally feel when I engage with peers in online discussion, I am able to learn and share ideas. Some examples are standards-based grading versus traditional grading, how much "tech" is too much for kids, the ideals of Postman, Turkle, and many other educational authors, as well as banning the use of mobile phones in schools.

That is my idea of professional development: the kind where I can present ideas to peers and get almost instantaneous feedback.

GET INVOLVED! NO, BUT REALLY!

Carina Wong (2016) wrote *7 Ways Teachers are*

Connecting and Collaborating Online, and in it, said that teachers are doing *more* (shocker) to increase their visibility online.

Hosting that first webinar was a catalyst to the abundance of resources and people that I could have within my PLN, I only had to put myself out there and participate.

What can you do to collaborate with other educators and build your PLN online?

- ***Pick a social platform*** — it can be Twitter, Facebook, Instagram, blogging, etc. Whatever medium you are comfortable with but don't be afraid to jump out of your comfort zone!
- ***Take the time to PARTICIPATE!*** — Collaborate with other educators on various projects. You'd be surprised at the number of opportunities that are out there.
- ***Ask away*** — don't be afraid to ask questions. My very first time going live on Periscope was terrifying but asking questions after my experience made an even better second one for me.
- ***Create and share*** — In her article "Why Build Personal Learning Networks," author Sahana Chattopadhyay (2018) describes Harold Jarche's Personal Knowledge Management (PKM), which recommends that creating, re-creating, and sharing lead to continuous learning. Your PLN is your own personal learning and training network!

An Edutopia article by Vicki Davis (2015) stated: "Open networks like the PLN are profoundly impactful in the success of the modern professional."

When *Forbes* (Simmons, 2015) reported on a study of the impact of learning in open versus closed networks, they said:

> . . . according to multiple, peer reviewed studies, simply being in an open network instead of a closed one is the best predictor of career success . . . the further . . . you go towards a closed network, the more you repeatedly hear the same ideas, which reaffirm what you already believe. The further you go towards an open network, the more you're exposed to new ideas . . . in fact . . . half of the predicted difference in career success (i.e., promotion, compensation, industry recognition) is due to this one variable.

What is stopping you from collaborating, sharing, creating, and participating online? Growing a PLN can be intimidating, I know. The amount of effort you put into building and participating in it, however, you get back tenfold. By picking an out of the box (for you) platform, participating and engaging in conversations, asking questions, and creating and sharing your content and story, you are on your way to building a strong foundation for a successful PLN.

References

Bolger, K. Boone, S. Borowy, T. Clark, A (Producer). (2017). *From enraged to engaged: Using community circles to restore and empower students* [Video webinar]. https://zoom.us/recording/play/xrPpzTIPaLtFyd07f5Hs2kjNx8hy3TldY7cF22DuJ8MLfAa7QfTTaykgx0INoRS5

Chattopadhyay, S. (2018, March 13). Why build personal learning networks? https://elearningindustry.com/build-personal-learning-networks

Davis, V. (2015, November 11). Modern professional learning: Connecting PLCs with PLNs. https://www.edutopia.org/blog/modern-professional-learning-plc-pln-vicki-davis

Simmons, M. (2015, September 20). The no. 1 predictor of career success according to network science. https://www.forbes.com/sites/michaelsimmons/2015/01/15/this-is-the-1-predictor-of-career-success-according-to-network-science/#876e321e8290

TED. (2013, June 6). *Working together to make things happen* [Video file]. https://www.youtube.com/watch?v=Fd_nkBHgX8s

Wong, C. (2016, December 24). 7 Ways teachers are connecting and collaborating online. http://www.gettingsmart.com/2016/08/7-ways-social-media-is-changing-teaching/

[9]

WHAT THE HECK IS A PLN?

CHRISTINE DONNELLY

As I was sitting in my graduate classes at Loyola University, striving to learn ways to incorporate technology into classrooms so that it is meaningful and engaging for all students, I was awestruck at how much I didn't know. Here I thought I was young enough (yep, that's all it takes!) to be in the know about all of this great technology — I just needed strategies to use it in my math classroom. Each new class came with more information I was unaware of.

At first, I felt I was in over my head. I did my assignments merely to work towards graduation, as I needed my Master's Degree to keep my teaching license. Clearly, I knew so little that it wasn't worth trying to change everything about my teaching. I took some of the ideas learned and some of my assignments and made it applicable to my students. As hard as this is to admit, it wasn't until my second to last graduate class that I realized that even I could reach beyond my classroom and school for help with ideas, lessons, and implementing technology effectively.

It's called a PLN, although I had to look up that acronym too when my classmates were throwing it around like it was the most common thing ever. Professional Learning Networks (PLNs) have changed my ideas about teaching faster than any other thing I have experienced. PLNs are tools to connect, collaborate, create, and share with educators from around the world via technology and social media according to Tom Whitby in an article on PLNs in Edutopia (Whitby, 2013). As individuals, we all can get caught up in the patterns and mindsets of those around us, especially since those are often the only people we are able to see and talk to during the day. But connecting to others from different backgrounds with different experiences opens up your mind to so many bigger and better opportunities.

I am a self-proclaimed floater — in nine years of teaching, I have taught in three different school districts and three different schools. And while I have gained a lot of insight and don't regret any of my experiences, I think the monotony of my same lessons and same style of teaching (drill, homework check, exploration or notes, practice, repeat) got boring and made me itch for a change. I was like many teachers who dreaded professional learning days because very little came of it. And while this is true sometimes, I now know I have a whole world of outside resources to help revive my teaching and spark new ideas even if I am teaching the same content for the third year in a row.

IF I CAN DO IT, SO CAN YOU

I've always been good at connecting with people, I know that is part of the reason I am a good teacher (notice I say "good"…I'm working towards great). My students know I love them, I love math, and I love learning. I have always worked well with teachers, too. I co-plan with the best of them! I know I don't have all of the answers or the best lessons for every standard, but I do try new things and love getting ideas that will ignite my students' interest and curiosity. I wanted to find more engaging ways to teach my students math skills and how to learn independently. I kept hearing about connections people in my cohort were making with others outside of their schools.

My classmates and I got to know each other quickly, as we took classes together each week. We constantly discussed what we were doing in our classrooms and casually gave input to make lessons better. It was great conversation. Despite the fact that we saw each other every week, we connected on social media as well and met up for projects and coursework. I would see what they were doing in their classrooms via Twitter, Facebook, Pinterest, or I'd hear about it during presentations done through Zoom, Google Hangouts, or posted on Moodle (our learning management system). I was being bombarded but loved it. As I observed my classmates' postings on social media, I saw others they were connected to and started watching them as well.

I started doing some of my own research on PLNs. Was this something that people really seek out or just graduate students in a technology program? Quite a few articles came up in my basic Google search. Most were very simple, but spoke to its importance. Sara Bernard wrote an article that laid out five PLNs to check out that were already developed — a great starting point (Bernard, 2011). I also started noticing people referencing PLNs on Twitter. I had connected with another math teacher and he retweeted a graphic a member of his PLN on Twitter had created, dictating 10 reasons educators need PLNs. I wasn't on Twitter often but the topic was showing up everywhere, it seemed.

Twitter is a great place to connect to other educators I've found. I'll admit, at first I hated Twitter, but now it has connected me to so many educators and opened my eyes to so much information that I am hooked. Besides my cohort classmates, Twitter is where most of my PLN is at the moment. Keep in mind, this is all still new for me. I'm branching out slowly but surely, more so that I can stay on top of what I start. I have participated in a few Twitter chats (#msmathchat is one of my favorites), which has doubled the number of people I follow and who follow me. That's not many but it's a start. Trust me, anyone can do this, I am proof. Nine years of teaching and I'm just getting started. I feel refreshed and invigorated for the first time in a while. I've absolutely contemplated leaving the profession multiple times, but here it is, the end of June and I am excited for what next school year is going to look like.

So start with a Twitter chat or follow a hashtag, read a blog from someone who is merely reflecting on what is going on in his classroom, listen to a podcast on your way to work, or read a book put together by a bunch of awesome educators, who like you, just want to be better at their practice so every student has a fighting chance, then connect with them. No one is expected to do it all on their own, so why try?

DO IT FOR THE KIDS

You are great and you clearly you want what is best for your students, otherwise, you'd be reading something else. Besides the benefits for you as a teacher, imagine the feelings your students will have when their teacher is student-centered and ensuring that each has equal opportunity to grow. You know very well there are students you have taught who just push you to the edge, and you have run out of ideas for engaging them. We've all been there and we can help. We are charged to educate all students, but one person doesn't have the answers for students who come from all walks of life. But I may have the answer for one of your kiddos, and you may have the answer for one of mine so let's connect!

Think about the learning that will occur in your classroom and how you will be able to engage all of your students and brag on each one of them. In a 2016 KQED article by Janelle Bence, she discusses showing off student work online to add authenticity to student learning and share successes with other educators to hopefully benefit them (Bence, 2016). Over two years later, teachers are still using online platforms to show off work from their classrooms.

What student doesn't want their teacher to be so proud of their work that they share with the world? They will eat it up! Show them off (and your hard work too)! Your PLN isn't just for ideas and the preparation — they are there to cheer you and your students on as well. Therefore, take a chance and try something new.

I decided to take a chance in trying something new at the end of this year myself. A member of my PLN (and classmate of mine) said he would do a Mystery Zoom session with my class. He was going to call into my class and my students had to ask twenty yes or no questions to figure out where he was. Now, my preparation with them was less than good and it was the last day before summer break, but my students loved it! They asked questions during the call, and then I gave them a chance to get to know my classmate. The connection was great, and one I would not have made with them had I not had someone in my PLN willing to experiment with me. I have a lot to improve upon for next time, but with one under my belt, I feel much more confident about trying it again. Another cool thing about it is the other math teacher on my team came in to do the experience with us, and now has interest as well. I shared my experience on Twitter and have offers from others to participate next time, too.

I know there are times when it feels like teachers get stuck in their ways and don't want to try new things. While this may be true for some, there are people out there willing to create, collaborate, communicate, share, and reflect with you if you let them. Be the teacher you want to be, and find people who will be there with you and for you along the way. It won't only make you a better teacher, but your students will become better learners as well.

WHAT DO YOU HAVE TO LOSE?

Have I convinced you? Do you still feel like your classroom is an island confined by four walls? It's truly magical how much only a few connections can impact your profession, the one you chose because you were going to change the world for children. You still can; rekindle that fire. Many of my struggles as a teacher, the ones that have had me close to quitting more than once, seem a lot smaller because of the people I have connected with.

Building my PLN has enabled me to not have to start from scratch every day; it has helped me rid the feeling each new year of adding one more thing to my plate. My PLN has made teaching come alive again without me missing time with my husband or six-month-old baby. Building a PLN just made teaching feel possible again. You will no longer be an army of one. Find those who want to support you and create with you. There really is nothing like it.

References

Bence, J. (2017, March 09). *The Benefits of Sharing Student Work in Online Spaces.* Retrieved from https://ww2.kqed.org/education/2016/05/17/the-benefits-of-sharing-student-work-in-online-spaces/

Bernard, S. (2011, May 19). *5 Personal Learning Networks (PLNs) for Educators.* Retrieved from https://www.kqed.org/mindshift/11711/5-personal-learning-networks-plns-for-educators

Whitby, T. (2013, November 18). *How Do I Get a PLN?,* Retrieved from https://www.edutopia.org/blog/how-do-i-get-a-pln-tom-whitby

[10]

RIDING THE WAVE OF COMMUNITY

PATTIE HOLY-ILENDA

TESTING THE WATERS OF SOCIAL MEDIA

Just a few, short years ago, I found myself wading through the currents of Twitter and Facebook with my lifejacket firmly belted in place. You could say I was nervous in the Twittersphere and the murky depths of social media. Yet, I knew that there was so much to tap into that I would be missing out on in education and life by remaining stubbornly on shore. Still, was FOMO the real reason I found myself tweeting, or posting, or was it because I was intrigued by the interaction with others on the opposite end of my bandwidth? Hmm?

To be honest, I didn't know I needed a smartphone until I bought one, way behind others who by then were experts with them in their own right. The idea of using my phone to do anything other than making a phone call seemed odd. And now? I use my phone for so much more than I had ever thought possible. It is my lifeline for developing my

PLN, my professional learning network. Who knew that such a small device would open up worlds of possibilities to me in a few, short years? Who knew that I would gain so much from social networks and social media sites? Certainly not me!

SWIMMING LESSONS: THE EARLY DAYS OF TEACHING AND MY PLC

You see, back in the early nineties when I started teaching, my PLC consisted solely of peers and colleagues within my school. We relied heavily on each other and collaborated constantly. There was something magical about those early days of teaching when interdisciplinary units were the norm, not the exception. Looking back, I remember having so much fun as we dreamed up interactive, off-the-chain lessons that supported and reinforced what our students were learning in all classrooms, not just our own. The downside, however, to having such a tight-knit PLC was that it was just that. We didn't know what we didn't know. In a way that closeness contributed to a limited worldview.

When I moved to a brand-new school building six years into my career, my world and eyes opened up considerably. Suddenly, I had a fresh group of educators with whom I interacted who came from backgrounds different than my own. This enriched my life and caused me to stretch. I learned that my eyes and heart could be opened up so much more, which then helped me to interact with my students in ways I hadn't previously understood. Ultimately, I became a better teacher, as a result. Today, I am energized by my PLNs and PLCs on social networking sites, and like Marla Tabaka of Inc. said, I "seek out knowledge, inspiration, and great connections through them daily" (McLaughlin, 2015).

MY LIFE VEST: THE BENEFITS OF A HAVING AN ACTIVE PLN AND PLC

According to Torrey Trust (2012), "PLNs are teacher-driven, global-support networks that decrease isolation and promote independence." For me, the best part has been the decrease in isolation that I have felt as a veteran educator. In my experience, I have seen in my building the newbie-teachers gravitating toward each other. As a teacher of longer tenure, I have often found myself alone. However, in developing a broad PLN outside of my building, my self-esteem as an educator has been reaffirmed by colleagues, mentors, and experts in the field, and I am connected and built up once again.

Who knew that such a pairing of a smartphone and Twitter would transform my life as an educator, but it has! I never knew I needed either one to learn from before. Maybe, it is not fear of missing out that propels me to set my toe in the deep end, take a breath, and jump fully into the waters of social media. Maybe, it is the sincere desire to educate and make a difference in this world that moves me, and with my PLN I have what it takes to swim out to new shores.

DEEPER WATERS: HOW GRADUATE SCHOOL HAS FORTIFIED MY PLN

As an EdTech graduate student at Loyola University Maryland these last two years, I have done things I never thought possible and stretched my PLN to include individuals in other school districts and across the country. My Twitter feed includes experts who are making significant changes in education, and I look to them for insight, ideas, and, most importantly, for support. There is nothing like posting a tweet, only to find that a colleague in your PLN likes what you have to say, or is willing to offer respectful criticism. These interactions build me up and help me get stronger as I find my voice. For the first time, I have participated in Twitter chats, and even conducted one with my graduate peers. My current professor, Dr. Sarah Thomas, encourages us to publish our reflections, so I have started penning a blog called Posts By Pattie on BlogSpot: https://postsbypattie.blogspot.com. It's in its infancy, but I love writing it, as it gives me a chance to express to others what I am learning and to hear from them in return. I've even crafted a professional website portfolio as part of this graduate program, something I would never have done two years ago. Yes, the waters are deeper, but the tide is carrying me along to new places that I didn't know existed before developing my PLN.

One of the most important parts of this entire process has been how I, as an educator, have changed while expanding my PLN and my PLC. As Tammy Neil describes in her #EduMatch piece, "One Rural Teacher's Journey to

Passionate Teaching," I had come to twenty-something years of teaching only to find I had lost some of my passion, and I couldn't really put a finger on why. Like Tammy, I have regained my passion for teaching by purposefully interacting with other educators who have that special spark, that fire inside that ignites one to swim into the currents of lifelong learning. As this newfound energy burns more brightly within me, I have begun to look more toward my students for direction and insight, too, and the wave of energy has risen in me and my classroom like never before.

WAVES THAT RIPPLE FORTH: HELPING STUDENTS DEVELOP THEIR PLC

This school year, propelled by a group of amazing eighth graders and a talented educator who is an integral part of my PLC, Brianna Gibson, a group was formed in our school called S.O.C.A, Students of Color Achievers. S.O.C.A. came about because the students of color in our school felt not only invisible, but treated unfairly within our school community, and they wanted to do something positive to counteract their negative experiences. Brianna and I became their teacher advisors, and our classrooms their safe places. In coming together, Brianna, the students, and I listened to one another with open hearts and grappled with the harsh realities of racism. We had hard and necessary conversations. Students found their voices and made them heard. They also made original student films about the walls between us and the damage that racism causes. They, then, presented their films at the annual enrichment fair in May to the parents and students at our school. Throughout the year, we shared thoughts and experiences, enjoyed luncheons together, and even took a field trip. Sometimes we laughed; sometimes we cried. Together, though, we rebuilt the foundation of our school community so that all students felt safe and included.

As a result, S.O.C.A grew from less than a dozen students in October to nearly forty by the time June came around, with even more students expressing interest in participating next year. In the fall, we are looking to connect with the high school members of Delta Scholars and Alpha Achievers as mentors. We plan on developing our network to include leaders in the community for their wisdom and support, as well. Graduating eighth graders promised to come back from high school next year to help plan a world heritage night so that students, parents, teachers, and community members may share their cultures with one another. These students have changed my life as an educator forever, and I am profoundly grateful.

REFLECTING WATERS: LOOKING WITHIN

Had I not expanded my PLN and my PLC these past two years, I would never have known to look outside myself and have the confidence to swim with my students and help them build their own network. As strong as I feel being built up by my PLN and PLC, there is nothing more inspiring than a group of middle schoolers coming together, saying that something needs to change, and then actively taking the steps forward to change it. Not only do educators need a strong learning community and network, but students do, too. The sooner we come to this realization, the better our schools will become. The more purposefully we pave the way for student agency, the more that authentic community will occur, and lifelong learning will take place. So, I challenge you to dive into the deep end with the help of your PLN and PLC. The waters hold such magic, and riding the waves is like nothing else.

References

Crowley, B. (2014, December 31). 3 Steps for building a professional learning network. Retrieved May 25, 2018, from Education Week website: https://www.edweek.org/tm/articles/2014/12/31/3-steps-for-building-a-professional-learning.html

Fowler, D., & Riley, J. (2015, September 11). How to build your PLN on Twitter. Retrieved May 25, 2018, from The Journal website: https://thejournal.com/articles/2015/09/11/how-to-build-your-pln-on-twitter.aspx

Lavoie, T. (2017, June 1). Five ways to grow your PLN with Twitter. Retrieved May 25, 2018, from EdTalk website: http://blog.etechcampus.com/2017/06/01/five-ways-to-grow-your-pln-with-twitter/

McLaughlin, J. (2015, July 22). The differences between a PLN and PLC. Retrieved May 25, 2018, from Corwin Connect website: http://corwin-connect.com/2015/07/the-differences-between-a-pln-and-plc/

Neil, T. (2016). #EduMatch: Snapshot in Education (2016) (S. Thomas, Ed.). EduMatch.

Trust, T. (2012). Professional learning networks designed for teacher learning. Journal of Digital Learning in Teacher Education, 28(4). Retrieved from https://files.eric.ed.gov/fulltext/EJ972454.pdf

OTHER EDUMATCH TITLES

EduMatch Snapshot in Education (2016)

The #EduMatch Teacher's Recipe Guide Editors: Tammy Neil & Sarah Thomas

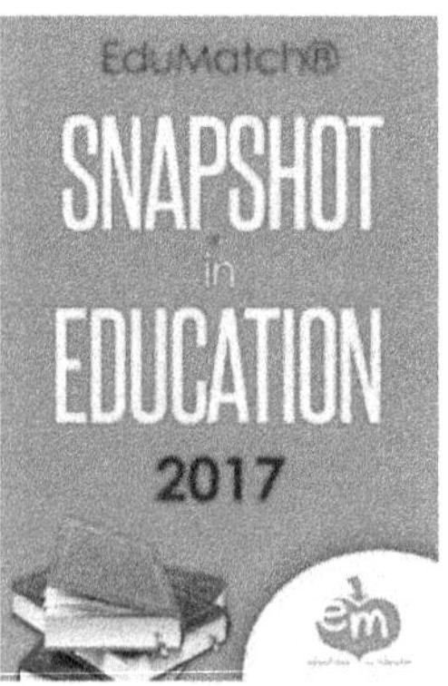

EduMatch Snapshot in Education (2017)

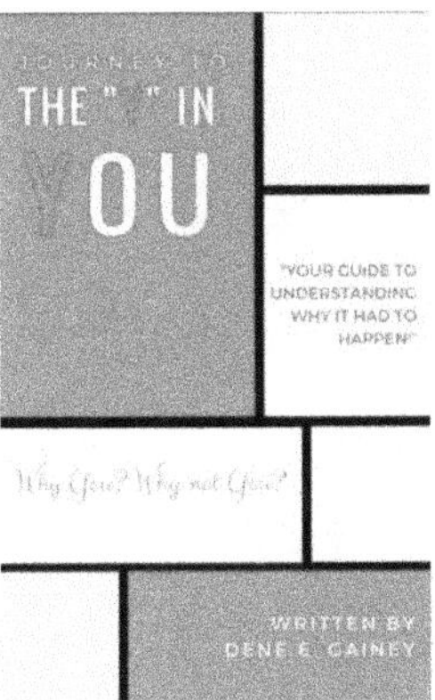

Journey to The "Y" in You by Dene Gainey

The Teacher's Journey by Brian Costello

The Fire Within Compiled and edited by Mandy Froehlich

EduMagic by Sam Fecich

Makers in Schools Editors: Susan Brown & Barbara Liedahl

Divergent EDU by Mandy Froehlich

EduMatch Snapshot in Education (2018)

Daddy's Favorites by Elissa Joy
Illustrated by Dionne Victoria

Level Up Leadership by Brian Kulak

DigCit Kids Editors: Marialice Curran & Curran Dee

Stories of EduInfluence by Brent Coley

The Edupreneur by Dr. Will

In Other Words… by Rachelle Dene Poth

One Drop of Kindness by Jeff Kubiak

em
EduMatch Publishing

www.ingramcontent.com/pod-product-compliance
Lightning Source LLC
Chambersburg PA
CBHW070644030426
42337CB00020B/4157
9781970133097